A BOOK ON PATENT DRAFTING FOR PATENT AGENT EXAMINATION 2023

ISERDINDIA ANALYTICS

Made with ♥ on the Notion Press Platform
www.notionpress.com

"To all those who work tirelessly to protect the rights of inventors and creators, this book is dedicated. May it serve as a comprehensive guide for those studying to become patent agents, helping them to safeguard the ideas that will drive progress and change."

Contents

Foreword

"As the field of patent law continues to evolve and grow, it is more important than ever to have well-trained and knowledgeable patent agents. This book, written by experienced patent agents, provides a comprehensive guide to the essential elements of patent drafting. From understanding the basics of patent law to drafting a clear and effective patent application, this book covers it all.

The Patent Agent Examination is a crucial step in becoming a successful patent agent, and this book is designed to help aspiring agents prepare for the exam. It covers the key topics and concepts that are tested on the exam, and provides clear and practical examples to illustrate key concepts.

We highly recommend this book to anyone studying for the Patent Agent Examination, or for anyone looking to deepen their understanding of the patent drafting process. It is an invaluable resource for anyone looking to protect the rights of inventors and creators, and to safeguard the ideas that will shape our world."

Preface

"As patent agents, we understand the importance of having a thorough understanding of the patent drafting process. From understanding the basics of patent law to drafting a clear and effective patent application, the ability to navigate the complexities of the patent system is essential.

This book is designed to help aspiring patent agents, as well as inventors and creators, understand the essential elements of patent drafting. It covers the key topics and concepts that are tested on the Patent Agent Examination, and provides clear and practical examples to illustrate key concepts.

The book is divided into several chapters, each covering a different aspect of patent drafting, such as patentability, claims, specification and drawings, and more. The book also includes a section on common pitfalls and mistakes to avoid during the patent drafting process.

We hope this book will serve as a valuable resource for anyone studying for the Patent Agent Examination, or for anyone looking to deepen their understanding of the patent drafting process. It is our sincere desire that this book will assist you in protecting the rights of inventors and creators, and safeguarding the ideas that will shape our world."

Acknowledgements

"We would like to express our gratitude to all those who have contributed to the creation of this book. In particular, we would like to thank our colleagues and mentors who have shared their knowledge and experience with us, and have helped us to understand the complexities of patent law and the patent drafting process.

We are also grateful to our families and friends for their support and encouragement throughout the writing process. Without their unwavering support, this book would not have been possible.

We would also like to acknowledge the invaluable contributions of our editors and proofreaders, who have helped to ensure that this book is accurate, clear, and easy to understand.

Finally, we would like to extend our thanks to all the aspiring patent agents who have motivated us to write this book. May this book serve as a valuable resource in your journey towards becoming a successful patent agent."

Prologue

"In the fast-paced world of innovation and technology, protecting the rights of inventors and creators is more important than ever. The role of a patent agent is to navigate the complex world of patent law and to draft clear, effective patent applications that will safeguard the ideas that will shape our world.

As patent agents, we have seen firsthand the challenges that inventors and creators face when trying to protect their ideas. The patent drafting process can be daunting, and preparing for the Patent Agent Examination requires a deep understanding of the legal principles and technical concepts involved.

This book is designed to help aspiring patent agents and inventors navigate the complexities of patent law and the patent drafting process. It provides a comprehensive guide to the essential elements of patent drafting, including the basics of patent law, the patent application process, and the key concepts and topics tested on the Patent Agent Examination.

We hope that this book will serve as a valuable resource for anyone studying for the Patent Agent Examination, or for anyone looking to deepen their understanding of the patent drafting process. In the following pages, we will explore the complexities of patent law and the patent drafting process, providing practical examples and expert insights to help you succeed."

CHAPTER I

Patent Specification Writing

A patent specification is a document that describes an invention and how it works. It is an essential part of the patent application process, as it serves as the legal and technical foundation for the patent. A well-written patent specification can help ensure that the patent office understands the invention and that the patent is granted.

The purpose of a patent specification is to provide a written description of the invention that is clear, complete, and enabling. It should enable a person skilled in the relevant field to understand the invention and how to make and use it. The specification should also clearly define the boundaries of the invention and what is protected by the patent.

The patent specification consists of several parts, including a title, a field of invention, a background of the invention, the object of the invention, a summary of the invention, a brief description of the drawings, a detailed description of the invention, an abstract, and one or more claims.

The title of the invention should be a brief, descriptive phrase that accurately and concisely describes the nature of the invention.

The field of invention should describe the technical field to which the invention relates and any related art that may be relevant to understanding the invention.

The background of the invention should provide context for the invention and describe the problem that the invention solves.

The object of the invention should describe the purpose or goal of the invention.

The summary of the invention should provide a brief overview of the invention, including its key features and benefits.

The brief description of the drawings should describe any drawings included with the specification, such as diagrams or schematics.

The detailed description of the invention should provide a thorough and complete explanation of the invention, including how it works and how it can be made and used.

The abstract should provide a summary of the invention in a single paragraph. It should be a concise and factual description of the invention that is no longer than 150 words.

The claims define the scope of the invention and what is protected by the patent. They should be written in a clear and concise manner and should define the invention in terms of its technical features.

Finally, the specification should include any relevant drawings or diagrams that help illustrate the invention. These should be labeled and numbered, and should be referred to in the detailed description of the invention.

In conclusion, a patent specification is a critical component of the patent application process. It serves as the legal and technical foundation for the patent and should be written in a clear and concise manner that enables a person skilled in the relevant field to understand the invention and how to make and use it.

CHAPTER II

Identifying the Invention

Invention

An "invention" is a new product or process that solves a technical problem.

Example – Needing something not available (Calculator); Combining two or more products (Camera, Computer, Telephone); Applying a better understanding of nature (Velcro – nylon tapes).

Innovation

An application of better solutions that meet new requirements, unarticulated needs, or existing market needs.

Innovation

- Applying better solutions to problems
- Developing new solutions to problems
- New ways of delivering an existing service (e.g. telehealth)
- Finding new uses for existing technology / devices

What are not inventions?—

According to the Indian Patent Act, of 1970.

(a) an invention which is frivolous or which claims anything obviously contrary to well-established natural laws;

Some examples of frivolous nature and contrary to natural laws are:

- A Perpetual motion machine
- A machine alleged to be giving output without any input.
- A machine alleged to be giving 100% efficiency

(b) an invention the primary or intended use or commercial exploitation of which could be contrary public order or morality or which causes serious prejudice to human, animal or plant life or health or to the environment;

Some examples are:

- Any device/method/apparatus/machine for committing theft or gambling
- Any machine/method for counterfeiting the currency
- Any invention the use of which is found to be injurious to public health
- Any invention, intended use/commercial exploitation which is found to be injurious to public, animal, plant or health e.g. method of adulteration of food.
- Any invention, primary or intended use of which is likely to violate the well-accepted and settled social, cultural, legal norms of morality e.g. method of cloning of humans.
- Any invention the primary or proposed use of which would disturb the public order e.g. a device or a method for housebreaking.

(c) the mere discovery of a scientific principle or the formulation of an abstract theory or discovery of any living thing or non-living substance occurring in nature;

Explanation- Finding a new substance or a micro-organism occurring freely in nature is a discovery and not a patentable invention.

i. A claim for the discovery of scientific principle is not considered to be an invention, but when such a process is used with the manufacturing process resulting in a substance or an article may be considered to be an invention.

ii. A scientific theory is a statement about the natural world. These theories are not considered to be inventions no matter how radical or revolutionary insight they might provide since they do not result in a product or process. However, if the theory leads to practical application in the process of manufacture of an article or a substance it may well be patentable.

iii. Finding out that particular known material is able to withstand mechanical shock is a discovery and hence, not patentable.

Case Law

1. **In Bilski V. Kappos,** Justice Kennedy of the US Supreme Court said that "method of hedging risk in commodities trading is an abstract idea and thus not the patentable subject matter". In this case, Petitioner's patent application seeks protection for a claimed invention that explains how commodity buyers and sellers in the energy market can protect or hedge, against the risk of price changes. The concept of hedging is an unpatentable abstract idea just like algorithms **(2).**
2. **Benson & Flook. 'An idea by itself is not patentable'.**
3. **Rubber-Tip Pencil Co. V. Howard, 20 Wall. 498, 87 U.S. 507 (1874)**

(d) the mere discovery of a new form of a known substance which does not result in the enhancement of the known efficacy of that substance or the mere discovery of any new property or new use for a known substance or of the mere use of a known process, machine or apparatus unless such known process results in a new product or employs at least one new reactant.

Explanation.—For the purposes of this clause, salts, esters, ethers, polymorphs, metabolites, pure form, particle size, isomers, mixtures of isomers, complexes, combinations and other derivatives of known substance shall be considered to be the same substance, unless they differ significantly in properties with regard to efficacy;

The parliament enacted the standard of non-obviousness as the condition for patentability. Under this clause, the test of non-obviousness of an invention and discovery of the existence of significant enhancement in the efficacy (i.e., the ability to produce desired or intended result) of a substance are prerequisites of patentability. According to provisions the following are not inventions and hence, not patentable:

a. Mere discovery of a new form of a known substance which does not result in the enhancement of the known efficacy of that substance.
b. Mere discovery of any new property of a known substance
c. Mere discovery of a new use of a known substance
d. Mere use of known process unless such known process results in a new product or employs a new reactant
e. Mere use of a known machine or apparatus

Case Law

1. In a recent case in relation to a pharmaceutical substance, the Madras High Court holds that efficacy is therapeutic efficacy. The patent applicant is definitely aware as to what is the therapeutic effect of the drug for which a patent has already been taken and what is the difference between the therapeutic effect of the patented drug and the drug in which patent is asked for. Thus, Madras High Court, while interpreting Section 3(d) observed as follows: "If a discovery is made from a known substance, a duty is cast upon the patent applicant to show that the discovery has resulted in the enhancement of the known efficacy of the known substance. On such discovery, the explanation creates a deeming fiction that all derivatives of the known substance would be deemed to be the same unless it differs significantly in properties with regard to the efficacy". **(Novartis AG Vs Union of India W.S. 24760/06.**
2. **In Novartis AG Vs Union of India case,** the Supreme Court of India held that 'mere discovery of an existing drug would not amount to an invention'. The court further held that 'the Indian Patent Act for grant of pharmaceutical patents apart from proving the traditional tests of novelty, inventive step and application, there is a new test of enhanced therapeutic efficacy for claims that cover incremental changes to existing drugs which also Novartis's drug did not qualify'.

3. **In Ten Xc Wireless Inc & Anr vs Mobi Antenna Technologies,** the Delhi High Court held that 'a method of replacing the conventional antenna with split-sector antenna, and (ii) a split-sector asymmetric antenna for conventional antenna are all-mere uses of the asymmetric antenna already known. **Under Section 3 (d)** the subject claimed is therefore not an invention. (2)

(e) a substance obtained by a mere admixture resulting only in the aggregation of the properties of the components thereof or a process for producing such substance;

(f) the mere arrangement or re-arrangement or duplication of known devices each functioning independently of one another in a known way;

Case Law

1. An invention claiming a mere juxtaposition of known devices in which each device functions independently is not considered patentable. Merely placing side by side old integers so that each performs its own function independently of others is not a patentable combination (for example- a flour mill provided by sieving means). However, where the old integers when placed together have some working interrelation producing a new or improved result, then there could be a patentable subject matter in the working interrelation brought about by the collection of integers. When two or more features of an apparatus are known, and they are juxtaposed without any interdependence on their functioning, they should be held to have been already known. **(Rampratap v. Bhabha Atomic Research Centre, 1976 IPLR 28 P.35), e.g. an umbrella with fan (388/Bom/73), bucket attached with a torch, clock and transistor in a single cabinet.**
2. A new combination may be the subject matter of the patent although every part of the combination per se is old, for here the new article is the part themselves but the assembling and working of the parts together. The merit of the new combination very much depends upon the result produced. Where the slight alteration turns that which was practically useless into what is important and useful, it is a fit subject matter for the patent. **(Lallubhai Chakubhai v. Shamaldas Sankalchand Shah AIR 1934 Bom 407).(2)**

(g) Omitted by the Patents (Amendment) Act, 2002

(h) a method of agriculture or horticulture;

(i) any process for the medicinal, surgical, curative, prophylactic [2]diagnostic, therapeutic or other treatment of human beings or any process for a similar treatment of animals to render them free of disease or to increase their economic value or that of their products.

(j) plants and animals in whole or any part thereof other than microorganisms but including seeds, varieties and species and essentially biological processes for production or propagation of plants and animals;

(k) a mathematical or business method or a computer programme per se or algorithms;

(l) a literary, dramatic, musical or artistic work or any other aesthetic creation whatsoever including cinematographic works and television productions;

(m) a mere scheme or rule or method of performing mental act or method of playing game;

(n) a presentation of information;

(o) topography of integrated circuits;

(p) an invention which in effect, is traditional knowledge or which is an aggregation or duplication of known properties of a traditionally known component or components.

Case Law

Traditional Knowledge is important to have a cultural orientation or based on culture and is important for the cultural identity of the group. Pharmaceutical patents are granted which are meant to be revoked once the patent invention was compared to the teaching of traditional knowledge consisting of prior art (for example-Antiseptic properties of Turmeric for wound healing, and pesticidal and insecticidal properties of Neem is not a patentable invention). The case of the revocation of the patent granted to **W.R. Grace Company and US Department of Agriculture (EPO Patent No. 436 257)** by European Patent Office on the grounds of not the presence of 'novelty' and the innovation being used in the country India for centuries. (2)

Inventions relating to atomic energy not patentable

No patent shall be granted in respect of an invention relating to atomic energy falling within subsection (1) of section 20 of the Atomic Energy Act, 1962 (33 of 1962).

Patentability Criteria for an Invention to be Patented

Patent law provides protection for inventions that meet certain requirements, known as patentability criteria. In this chapter, we will explore the three main patentability criteria that an invention must meet in order to be eligible for patent protection.

Novelty

The first patentability criteria is novelty, which means that the invention must be new and not previously disclosed in any form to the public before the filing of the patent application. This includes any prior art, such as previous patents, publications, or public disclosures.

The novelty requirement helps to ensure that the patent system promotes innovation by providing protection for new and useful inventions, while also preventing the patenting of inventions that are already known to the public.

Non-Obviousness

The second patentability criteria is non-obviousness, which means that the invention must not be obvious to a person having ordinary skill in the relevant field of the invention. This requirement helps to prevent the patenting of inventions that are obvious variations or combinations of known elements, and promotes innovation by providing protection for truly novel and non-obvious inventions.

Utility

The third patentability criteria is utility, which means that the invention must have some practical application or utility. This requirement helps to ensure that the patent system promotes innovation by providing protection for inventions that have some real-world application or use.

In addition to these three main patentability criteria, there are also other requirements that an invention must meet in order to be eligible for patent protection, such as the requirement for a written description, enablement, and best mode.

It is important to note that patentability criteria varies from country to country and region to region, so it is advisable to consult a patent attorney or agent in order to determine whether an invention meets the specific patentability criteria in the country where patent protection is sought.

Additional Criteria

In addition to the three main patentability criteria, there are several other criteria that an invention must meet in order to be eligible for patent protection. These include:

Written description: The patent application must provide a written description of the invention that is sufficiently detailed to enable a person having ordinary skill in the relevant field of the invention to understand and make the invention.

Enablement: The patent application must provide enough information to enable a person having ordinary skill in the relevant field of the invention to understand and make the invention.

Best mode: The patent application must disclose the best mode of carrying out the invention known to the inventor at the time of filing the application.

It is important to consult with a patent attorney or agent to ensure that an invention meets all of the patentability criteria and other requirements for patent protection.

What are the subjects of a Patent?

A patent is a legally-binding grant of exclusive rights to an inventor for a limited period of time, in exchange for the public disclosure of the details of the invention. However, not all inventions are eligible for patent protection. In order for an invention to be considered for patent protection, it must fall under one of the following categories of subjects:

Mechanical devices and articles of manufacture

Mechanical devices and articles of manufacture are a category of subjects that are eligible for patent protection under the laws of most countries. This category includes machines, tools, and other mechanical devices, as well as manufactured articles such as clothing and household goods.

Examples of mechanical devices and articles of manufacture that may be eligible for patent protection include:

- A new design for a bicycle
- A new type of engine
- A new type of clothing fastener
- A new type of kitchen appliance
- A new type of medical instrument
- A new type of sporting equipment

To be eligible for patent protection, a mechanical device or article of manufacture must meet certain requirements, including being novel and non-obvious, and being useful. The invention must be new and not previously disclosed in any form to the public before the filing of the patent application. The invention must also not be obvious to a person having ordinary skill in the relevant field of the invention. Finally, the invention must have some practical application or utility.

It's also worth noting that in some cases, the patent office may require a working model of the invention to be submitted with the patent application in order to demonstrate that the invention is useful.

Additionally, some countries may have specific laws or regulations regarding patentable subject matter for mechanical devices and articles of manufacture, so it's important to consult with a patent attorney with knowledge of your country's laws to determine whether your invention is eligible for patent protection.

Processes and methods

Processes and methods are another category of subjects that are eligible for patent protection under the laws of most countries. This category includes any process or method that can be used to make or use a product or perform a particular task. Examples of processes and methods that may be eligible for patent protection include:

- Manufacturing processes, such as a new process for producing a chemical compound or a new method for constructing a building
- Business methods, such as a new method for conducting financial transactions or a new method for organizing a company's supply chain
- Software algorithms, such as a new algorithm for image compression or a new method for encrypting data
- Medical methods, such as a new surgical procedure or a new treatment method

To be eligible for patent protection, a process or method must meet certain requirements, including being novel and non-obvious, and being useful. The invention must be new and not previously disclosed in any form to the public before the filing of the patent application. The invention must also not be obvious to a person having ordinary skill in the relevant field of the invention. Finally, the invention must have some practical application or utility.

It's also worth noting that certain types of methods or process may be excluded from patent protection in some countries, for example methods for medical treatments, methods for performing purely mental steps, and methods for playing games.

Additionally, some countries may have specific laws or regulations regarding patentable subject matter for processes and methods, so it's important to consult with a patent attorney with knowledge of your country's laws to determine whether your invention is eligible for patent protection.

Chemical compositions or compounds

Chemical compositions or compounds are another category of subjects that are eligible for patent protection under the laws of most countries. This category includes any chemical composition or compound, including pharmaceuticals, fertilizers, and other chemical products. Examples of chemical compositions or compounds that may be eligible for patent protection include:

- New chemical compounds, such as a new drug molecule or a new type of fertilizer
- New uses for existing chemical compounds, such as a new medical treatment using a known drug molecule
- New methods for synthesizing chemical compounds, such as a new method for producing a known drug molecule

To be eligible for patent protection, a chemical composition or compound must meet certain requirements, including being novel and non-obvious, and being useful. The invention must be new and not previously disclosed in any form to the public before the filing of the patent application. The invention must also not be obvious to a person having ordinary skill in the relevant field of the invention. Finally, the invention must have some practical application or utility.

It's also worth noting that some countries may have specific laws or regulations regarding patentable subject matter for chemical compounds, for example some countries may require that the compound is novel, non-obvious, and useful, and that it is fully and clearly described in the patent application.

Additionally, in some countries, certain types of chemical compounds may be excluded from patent protection, for example natural compounds, and some countries may have specific laws or regulations regarding patentable subject matter for chemical compounds, so it's important to consult with a patent attorney with knowledge of your country's laws to determine whether your invention is eligible for patent protection.

Isolated and characterized molecules

Isolated and characterized molecules are a subcategory of chemical compositions or compounds that are eligible for patent protection under the laws of most countries. This subcategory includes any molecules that have been isolated from their natural source and characterized, such as DNA, RNA, and proteins. Examples of isolated and characterized molecules that may be eligible for patent protection include:

- Isolated genes, such as a new gene related to a specific disease
- Isolated proteins, such as a new enzyme
- Isolated RNA, such as a new ribozyme

To be eligible for patent protection, an isolated and characterized molecule must meet certain requirements, including being novel and non-obvious, and being useful. The invention must be new and not previously disclosed in any form to the public before the filing of the patent application. The invention must also not be obvious to a person having ordinary skill in the relevant field of the invention. Finally, the invention must have some practical application or utility.

It's worth noting that certain types of isolated and characterized molecules may be excluded from patent protection in some countries, for example naturally occurring DNA, RNA and proteins, and some countries may have specific laws or regulations regarding patentable subject matter for isolated and characterized molecules, so it's important to consult with a patent attorney with knowledge of your country's laws to determine whether your invention is eligible for patent protection.

Genetic organisms and gene sequences

Genetic organisms and gene sequences are another category of subjects that are eligible for patent protection under the laws of most countries. This category includes any genetically modified organism (GMO) or gene sequences that have been modified through genetic engineering techniques. Examples of genetic organisms and gene sequences that may be eligible for patent protection include:

- Transgenic plants, such as a new type of corn or soybean that has been genetically modified to resist pests
- Transgenic animals, such as a new type of mouse that has been genetically modified to model a specific disease
- Synthetic DNA sequences, such as a new gene that has been engineered to produce a specific protein

To be eligible for patent protection, a genetic organism or gene sequence must meet certain requirements, including being novel and non-obvious, and being useful. The invention must be new and not previously disclosed in any form to the public before the filing of the patent application. The invention must also not be obvious to a person having ordinary skill in the relevant field of the invention. Finally, the invention must have some practical application or utility.

It's also worth noting that certain types of genetic organisms or gene sequences may be excluded from patent protection in some countries, for example naturally occurring genetic organisms or gene sequences, and some countries may have specific laws or regulations regarding patentable subject matter for genetic organisms or gene sequences, so it's important to consult with a patent attorney with knowledge of your country's laws to determine whether your invention is eligible for patent protection.

Computer programs

Computer programs are another category of subjects that are eligible for patent protection under the laws of most countries. This category includes any software or program that is written in any programming language, such as C++, Java, or Python. Examples of computer programs that may be eligible for patent protection include:

- Operating systems, such as a new type of mobile operating system
- Business software, such as a new type of accounting software
- Gaming software, such as a new video game
- Mobile apps, such as a new type of social media app
- Artificial intelligence software, such as a new machine learning algorithm

To be eligible for patent protection, a computer program must meet certain requirements, including being novel and non-obvious, and being useful. The invention must be new and not previously disclosed in any form to the public before the filing of the patent application. The invention must also not be obvious to a person having ordinary skill in the relevant field of the invention. Finally, the invention must have some practical application or utility.

It's worth noting that in some countries, the laws related to patent protection for computer programs may vary, for example, in some countries, computer programs may be considered as a form of literary work and may be protected under copyright law instead of patent law. In addition, certain elements of a computer program, such as mathematical algorithms, may not be eligible for patent protection. So it's important to consult with a patent attorney with knowledge of your country's laws to determine whether your invention is eligible for patent protection.

Improvements

Improvements refer to modifications or advancements made to existing inventions that are eligible for patent protection. These can include new features, new methods of using an existing invention, new materials or design changes. Examples of improvements that may be eligible for patent protection include:

- Improvements to a mechanical device, such as a new gear design for a bicycle
- Improvements to a process or method, such as a new method of manufacturing a specific product
- Improvements to a chemical composition or compound, such as a new formulation of a pharmaceutical drug
- Improvements to an isolated and characterized molecule, such as a new variation of a protein
- Improvements to a computer program, such as a new user interface for a mobile app

To be eligible for patent protection, an improvement must meet certain requirements, including being novel and non-obvious, and being useful. The invention must be new and not previously disclosed in any form to the public before the filing of the patent application. The invention must also not be obvious to a person having ordinary skill in the relevant field of the invention. Finally, the invention must have some practical application or utility. It's also worth noting that in order to be considered an improvement, the invention must be different enough from the existing invention that it is considered to be a new and distinct invention.

It's important to note that the laws and regulations surrounding the patentability of improvements can vary depending on the country or region, so it is best to consult with a patent attorney with knowledge of your country's laws to determine whether your invention is eligible for patent protection.

It is important to note that not all inventions will fall under these categories, and some may fall under multiple categories. Additionally, the laws and regulations regarding patentable subject matter may vary from country to country.

When considering whether to seek patent protection for an invention, it is important to conduct a thorough prior art search to determine whether the invention is novel and non-obvious, and to consult with a patent attorney to determine whether the invention is eligible for patent protection.

One of the most important steps in the patent specification writing process is identifying the invention. This involves clearly and concisely defining the technical features of the invention and how it is novel and non-obvious.

The first step in identifying the invention is to determine the technical field to which it belongs. This will help to narrow the focus of the specification and ensure that it is directed to the appropriate audience.

Next, it is important to consider the prior art. Prior art refers to any information that was publicly available before the date of the invention. This can include patents, published papers, and other written or publicly disclosed materials. It is important to consider the prior art because an invention must be novel and non-obvious in order to be eligible for a patent. This means that it must not be anticipated by the prior art or be an obvious extension of what is already known.

Once the technical field and the relevant prior art have been considered, the next step is to clearly define the technical features of the invention. This involves describing the structure, function, and operation of the invention in detail. It is important to be as specific and detailed as possible, as this will help to clearly define the boundaries of the invention and what is protected by the patent.

It is also important to consider how the invention is novel and non-obvious in light of the prior art. This can involve comparing the technical features of the invention to the prior art and explaining how the invention differs and how it provides a new and useful solution to a technical problem.

In conclusion, identifying the invention is a critical step in the patent specification writing process. It involves defining the technical features of the invention, considering the prior art, and explaining how the invention is novel and non-obvious. By clearly and concisely identifying the invention, it will be easier to obtain a patent and protect the rights of the inventor.

CHAPTER III

Disclosing the Invention

Once the invention has been identified, the next step in the patent specification writing process is disclosing the invention. This involves describing the invention in sufficient detail that a person skilled in the relevant field can understand how it works and how to make and use it.

The disclosure of the invention should be clear, concise, and complete. It should include a detailed description of the structure, function, and operation of the invention, as well as any relevant drawings or diagrams.

It is important to be as specific and detailed as possible when disclosing the invention. This will help to clearly define the boundaries of the invention and what is protected by the patent. It will also make it easier for a person skilled in the relevant field to understand the invention and replicate it.

It is also important to consider the prior art when disclosing the invention. The disclosure should explain how the invention is novel and non-obvious in light of the prior art and should include any relevant comparisons to the prior art.

In conclusion, disclosing the invention is a critical step in the patent specification writing process. It involves describing the invention in sufficient detail that a person skilled in the relevant field can understand how it works and how to make and use it. By clearly and concisely disclosing the invention, it will be easier to obtain a patent and protect the rights of the inventor.

CHAPTER IV

Title of Invention

The title of an invention, also known as the invention title, is a brief statement that describes the general nature of the invention. The title is usually included at the top of the patent application, and it serves as a quick reference for the patent office and others who may be reviewing the application.

The title should be concise and accurately describe the invention. It should be specific enough to distinguish the invention from other similar inventions, but not so specific that it limits the scope of the invention. The title should not include any legal or claim language, and it should not include any trade names or trademarks.

The title of an invention is a brief, descriptive phrase that accurately and concisely describes the nature of the invention. It should be easy to understand and should not be too long or too technical.

The title should be chosen carefully, as it will be used to identify the invention and distinguish it from other inventions in the same technical field. It should be unique and should not be too similar to the titles of other patents or published materials.

The title should also accurately and concisely describe the technical features of the invention. It should be specific enough to clearly identify the invention, but general enough to cover all possible variations and applications of the invention.

It is important to note that the title does not have any legal significance and does not affect the scope of the claims. It is important to choose a title that is accurate, but also broad enough that it does not limit the scope of the claims. This is because the title is only used for administrative purposes and does not affect the scope of the claims.

When drafting the title, it is important to consider the audience for whom the title is intended. The title should be easily understood by someone with a general understanding of the field of the invention, but not so general that it fails to distinguish the invention from other similar inventions.

In conclusion, the title of an invention is an important part of the patent specification. It should be chosen carefully and should accurately and concisely describe the nature of the invention. By choosing a clear and descriptive title, it will be easier to identify and distinguish the invention from other inventions in the same technical field.

According to section 10 (1) of the Patents Act, 1970. "Title" should be sufficiently indicating the subject matter to which the invention relates. Rule 13 (7) (a) requires title to disclose the specific features of the invention normally in not more than fifteen words. Though in practice, very rarely objections have been raised based on title being non-indicative, it's always recommended to write an indicative title in less than fifteen words. Title should not contain any Irrelevant or other matter not necessary for the elucidation of the Invention. Further, title should be free from fancy expressions and ambiguities. Some terms that should be avoided in a title are: - a. Inventor's name b. The word "Patent" c. Words in other languages d. Usage of Abbreviations such as "etc." e. Fancy words such as "Best Furniture"

The title may allude to the claimed invention but it is not supposed to recite the invention. Thus if the claims recite use of a novel class of polymers in automobile tyres the 'Title' may be properly worded as 'Polymers containing" and their use in Automobile tyres or Automobile tyre methods and compositions depending on the focus of the claims. Numeration is important in the title as elsewhere in the application. For example, it's better to say that "Methods and Apparatus for cleaning Teeth" than "Method and Apparatus for cleaning Teeth'

It is also important to consider the keywords used in the title as it can help to increase the visibility of the patent application during a patent search.

A few best practices to keep in mind while drafting the title are:

- Keep the title brief and concise.
- Make sure the title accurately describes the invention.
- Avoid using legal or claim language.
- Avoid using trade names or trademarks.

• Consider the audience and the keywords used in the title.

Example of a title: "System and method for detecting and preventing cyber attacks on a computer network"

In conclusion, the title of an invention is an important part of a patent application, as it provides a quick reference for the patent office and others who may be reviewing the application. The title should be concise, accurate, and easy to understand, and should not include any legal or claim language. It is important to consider the audience and the keywords used in the title to increase the visibility of the patent application during a patent search.

Draft the appropriate Title for the following abstract:

1. A toothbrush include cleaning element support members that enhance cleaning and user comfort while brushing. The cleaning element support member permit a head of toothbrush to be comfortably received and manipulated within the user head. Each flexible cleaning element support member has flexible stem formed of a resilient material.

Ans: Enhanced Comfort Toothbrush with Resilient Cleaning Element Support Members

2. Control over access by individual to a group of high security facilities and zones within such facilities is accomplished with use of biometric reader at each access door as well as a quick id reading device that is not required to contain biometric information. The individual allowed security facility at a given time and also control their own schedule.

Ans: Biometric and Quick ID Access Control System for High Security Facilities and Zones

3. A diagnostic test system having a portable testing device for motor vehicles, controllers having an on- board diagnostic device being provided which control and monitor the engine control system and other system of vehicle. The external portable testing device is equipped with modem connected to mobile, in order to perform error diagnosis and troubleshooting network outside stationary repair shops.

Ans: Portable Diagnostic Test System with Modem Connectivity for Motor Vehicles

4. The invention relates to a device and system for preventing in proper use of car. The device uses a electronically controlled fuel system to cut off system located internally of fuel tank. The system of car required a user to enter a specific pin number in order to operate the vehicle. Upon writing secret code by law enforcement officer, the circuit board stop the supply of current to fuel shut off system and shutting down the engine.

Ans: Device and System for Preventing Improper Use of Car

5. A wearable mobile computing device with high resolution display that is capable of wireless accessing information from a network and a variety of other devices.it use a user interface that is used to efficiently interact with alarms and notifications on watch.

Ans: Wearable Mobile Computing Device with High Resolution Display and Efficient User Interface

6. There is disclosed a strong rack that can on load, secure, and offload a human transporter device such as SEGWAY. The Ramp is secured to the storage rack in upright position when the caring vehicle is in motion.

Ans: Strong Rack for Loading, Securing, and Offloading Human Transporter Device

7. A very light, very small carbon fibre composite hull, simple passenger Formula-One-form-factor, flex-fuel, plug-in hybrid with swappable battery packs. The car will have very low drag as Formula-One front and rear aerodynamics wing will be extended to cover open wheel to reduce Vortices. These will also be covered with solar panels to provide partial trickle charge while car is in the sun while parked at work etc.

Ans: Compact Carbon Fiber Hybrid with Swappable Batteries and Solar Panels

8. A method and apparatus for periodically and automatically testing ans monitoring the blood glucose level. A disposable testing unit is carried by the patient's body and has a testing chamber in fluid communication with infusion lines and a catheter connected to patient blood vessel. A reversible peristaltic pump pumps the infusion fluid forwardly in the patient blood vessel. The presence of blood in testing chamber is detected by LED/ photo-detector pairs. The resulting glucose level is shown in monitor. The unit is typically used for a patient in an intensive care unit.

Ans: Automatic Blood Glucose Testing and Monitoring Method and Apparatus with Disposable Testing Unit

9. An article of footwear for use of playing soccer or any other sport that require kicking of ball by player's feet. The ball controlled region is formed by three interrelated layers each layer is formed of a separate material with distinct function. The outer layer is formed by material which easily compress and attract and slow the ball speed.

The core layer is comprised of high tensile metal or plastic to provide a player with extra power and energy during power kicks. Further, the layers of the ball control region act in unison to allow player to achieve a variety of desired effects on ball.

Ans: Soccer Footwear with Three-Layer Ball Control Region for Improved Kicking Performance

10. A two-wheel battery-powered vehicle has a platform and two wheels connected to the platform, wherein a battery-powered wheel drives the wheel. An attachment is connected to the platform and a sensor device is arranged in the platform. A person standing on the platform and engaging the attachment moves the platform into angle position corresponding to a body position of person. The attachment has a leg support device for at least one leg of person standing on platform for keeping the platform at a desired angle position.

Ans: Two-Wheel Battery-Powered Vehicle with Platform Angle Control and Leg Support Attachment

CHAPTER V

Field of Invention

I. Introduction

The field of invention refers to the area or technical domain to which an invention belongs. Properly identifying the field of invention in a patent application is important because it helps to provide context and background information about the invention, as well as to establish its relevance and potential impact.

The field of invention refers to the area of technology to which the invention pertains. It is important to clearly define the field of invention in a patent application as it helps to establish the context in which the invention should be considered and evaluated. The field of invention is typically included in the background section of a patent specification and it is used to provide a general overview of the area of technology to which the invention pertains.

When defining the field of invention, it is important to be specific and to use technical terms that are commonly used in the relevant area of technology. This can help to establish the context in which the invention should be considered and evaluated. It is also important to provide a brief overview of the state of the art in the field of invention, which can include a description of the current problems, limitations, and challenges that exist in the field.

It is also important to include information about any related prior art references that are relevant to the field of invention. These can include patents, publications, and other technical documents that pertain to the field of technology in which the invention is being developed. This information can be used to show the novelty and non-obviousness of the invention and to establish the context in which the invention should be considered and evaluated.

When writing the field of invention, it is also important to avoid including any information that may limit the scope of the invention or that may be considered as prior art. This can include information about the invention's specific features, limitations, or objectives, as these can be discussed in other sections of the patent specification.

It is also important to keep the field of invention brief, concise, and easy to understand. This can help to ensure that the patent application is clear, readable, and informative.

In summary, the field of invention is an important part of a patent application that helps to establish the context in which the invention should be considered and evaluated. It is important to be specific and to use technical terms that are commonly used in the relevant area of technology, to provide a brief overview of the state of the art in the field of invention, and to include information about any related prior art references that are relevant to the field of invention. It is also important to avoid including any information that may limit the scope of the invention or that may be considered as prior art, and to keep the field of invention brief, concise, and easy to understand.

II. Determining the Field of Invention

There are several factors to consider when determining the field of invention for an invention. These include:

- The technical area or industry in which the invention is used or applied
- The specific problem or need that the invention addresses
- The technical features or characteristics of the invention

For example, an invention that is a new type of medical device used to treat a specific medical condition would belong to the field of medical devices and treatment of the specific medical condition. An invention that is a new type of software program used to perform a specific task would belong to the field of computer software and the specific task it performs.

III. Importance of the Field of Invention in Patent Prosecution

Accurately disclosing the field of invention in a patent application is important because it can impact the novelty and non-obviousness of the invention. In order to be eligible for a patent, an invention must be novel and non-obvious in the field of invention. This means that it must not be anticipated by prior art in the same field, and it must not be an obvious extension.

This section should preferably begin with a short general statement about the invention that shows the scope of the invention and indicates briefly the technology area to which the invention applies.

Use the phrase "The present invention relates to the field of......... and, in particular, relates to ...(subfield)....".

First section of the field should broadly cover the invention area and subfield section should be narrow.

For example, the present invention relates to the field of advertisement and, in particular, relates to bidding for advertisements.

The statement should preferably begin with "The invention relates to...". This section can then further describe the applicable technology area at a higher level of detail. For instance, the field of invention section can be written as "The invention relates to a novel biodegradable polymer additive composition useful for the preparation of biodegradable plastic products and a process for the preparation of the said composition. The invention, more particularly, relates to a novel biodegradable polymer composition, which is useful for the preparation of a biodegradable master batch composition, which in turn is useful for the preparation of a biodegradable polymer profile useful for the manufacture of biodegradable products such as Carrier bags, Garbage Disposal Bags, Hospital Disposables, Packaging Film and Thermoformed Plastics."

Details of the invention should be avoided in this section. The field of the invention should be defined in general terms and should not contain any language that may be interpreted to limit the scope of protection.

The field of the invention should be carefully chosen to balance among competing consideration. On the other hand, the fields should be sufficiently broad to encompass all contemplated embodiments of the claimed invention. For example, if it has been discovered that a particular ceramic is useful for filing dental cares, the field may properly be worded as 'dentistry'. But if the inventors contemplate that the ceramic may also be used for filing voids in bone repair including orthopaedics and density. Still further, if the ceramic itself comprises the principal novelty the field is more properly worded as 'medical ceramics' or merely 'ceramics'. Some more examples like The following invention relates tea process or the invention relates to a product or the invention relates to a novel herbal formulation etc. Thereafter, the advantages of the invention may be mentioned to bring out clearly the areas of application and preferable use of the invention. The applicant may substantiate industrial applicability of the invention in this part.

CHAPTER VI

Background of Invention

The State of the art section, also known as the Background of Invention, is an important component of the patent specification. It demonstrates the primary need for an invention and provides a basic context for the invention. The section discusses the existing problem that the invention proposes to solve and includes all previous works that have attempted to solve the problem. It highlights the status of technology in the field of the invention and focuses on identifying patents, experiments, publications, journals, and pending patent applications in the specific field. All this information is collectively referred to as prior art.

The background of invention is a section in a patent application that provides a general context for the invention. It includes information about the state of the art in the field of the invention and describes any prior art references that are relevant to the invention. This section is important because it helps to establish the novelty of the invention and explain why the invention is needed.

The background of invention is typically divided into two parts: a general background section and a specific background section. The general background section provides a broad overview of the field of the invention and the specific background section provides more detailed information about the prior art references that are relevant to the invention.

In the general background section, it is important to provide a brief overview of the field of the invention and explain how the invention fits into the field. This section should also describe any technical problems or challenges that exist in the field and explain how the invention addresses those problems.

The specific background section should provide a detailed description of the prior art references that are relevant to the invention. This section should include information about the prior art references such as their titles, authors, and publication dates. It should also describe the technical features of the prior art references and explain how they differ from the invention.

It is also important to note any disadvantages or shortcomings of the prior art references and how the invention overcomes them. This helps to establish the novelty and non-obviousness of the invention.

When writing the background of invention, it is important to use clear and concise language and avoid using jargon or technical terms that may be difficult for non-experts to understand. It is also important to be as objective as possible when describing the prior art references and to avoid making negative or derogatory statements about the prior art.

In addition, the last paragraph of the background should highlight the need of present invention to overcome the disadvantages of the prior arts and to provide certain benefits (without disclosing novelty). This last paragraph should start with the phrase "In light of the above stated discussion, there is a need of a method and system to ...."

In India, it is not necessary to specify the closest prior art in the background section. Describing prior arts in general is sufficient without specifically identifying them. Care must be taken as an acknowledgment of something as prior art may act as estoppels during the prosecution of the application.

When drafting the State of the art section, it's important to keep in mind a few effective strategies:

- Avoid using the term "Prior art" per se while describing the state of the art or anywhere in the patent specification.
- The state of the art section should not label anything as "the invention" while describing prior art(s). It should not be titled as "State of the art for the invention". Inclusion of the word invention may limit the interpretation of the inventive subject matter to the disclosed prior art.
- The state of the art should only highlight the problem that the invention solves. It should not be used to describe the solution of the identified problem.
- In cases where a substantial part of the invention is a discovery or recognition of a problem, the problem should be discussed in the "Detailed Description" section of the patent specification rather than in the state of the art.

- Care should be taken so that the state of the art does not limit the scope of the invention in any manner to any particular field of use.
- Even though the motive of the section is to knock-out all related prior art by describing its disadvantages, one should be careful not to use any derogatory statement for any prior art.

When drafting the background section, it's important to keep in mind a few do's and don'ts:
Do's:

- Double space after every line.
- Use 'System for', 'method for' instead of 'system of' and 'method of'
- If x contains a, b, c, etc. then use x includes a, b, c and the like.

Don'ts:

- Length of sentence should not exceed 2 lines.
- Don't use pronouns.
- Don't use informal words like 'etc.', 'i.e.'
- Don't use 'wherein', comprises'

In summary, it is important to remember the following when drafting the background of the invention:

- Do not tell novelty in the background.
- Do not use derogatory words for prior arts.
- Tell the disadvantages of prior art in terms of advantages of the present invention.
- Do not use pronouns.
- Do not use "wherein", "comprises"- in the background.
- Try to make a story.
- Paragraphs should not be more than 12-15 lines.
- In the first paragraph, try to cover the broad field of the invention.
- In the second paragraph, try to cover the subfield of the invention.

• To illustrate various prior art references, use:
In another Patent y, the system and method for ......(abstract from patent y with certain language modifications).
In yet another Patent z, the system and method for .... (abstract from patent z with certain language modifications).

• The last paragraph of the background should highlight the need of present invention to overcome the disadvantages of the prior arts and to provide certain benefits (without disclosing novelty). • Start the last paragraph with the phrase "In light of the above stated discussion, there is a need of a method and system to ...." This will help to emphasize the significance of the present invention in solving the problem identified in the background section.

It's also important to remember that the background section should be written in a clear and concise manner and should avoid any technical jargon that may be difficult for a layperson to understand. The section should also avoid using any language that may be interpreted as limiting the scope of the invention.

CHAPTER VII

The object of Invention

The object of an invention, also referred to as the objective of the invention, refers to what the invention aims to achieve. This section is crucial as it addresses the issue of obviousness and renders the invention as inventive and non-obvious over existing technology. It highlights the technical problems associated with the existing technology and aims to provide a solution by bringing out the differences between the invention and related prior art.

To write this section effectively, it is important to emphasize the main objective of the invention by repeating it time and again in order to clearly communicate it to the examiner. Additionally, it is recommended to discuss the advantages of the invention rather than the disadvantages of the prior art. This is because the disadvantages of the prior art have already been discussed in detail in the "state of the art" section and reciting them again would make the specification look verbose and repetitive.

In order to clearly convey the solution sought by the invention, it is important to include statements such as "It has already been proposed..." followed by the object(s) which the invention has in view, e.g., "The principal object of the invention is...", "Another object of the invention is...", "A further object of the invention is...", etc.

It is also important to remember that the object of the invention should be specific and not too broad. This is because a broad statement of the object of the invention may be considered obvious and may not be considered patentable.

When describing this section, it's important to keep in mind a few effective strategies:

- Emphasize on the main objective of the invention by repeating it time and again. This will help to effectively sell the invention to the examiner.
- Discuss more the advantages of the invention rather than the disadvantages of the prior art. Disadvantages of the prior art have already been discussed in detail in the "state of the art" section and reciting them again would make the specification look verbose and repetitive.
- Try to provide a clear and concise explanation of the problem that the invention solves and the benefits it provides. Avoid using technical jargon that may be difficult for a layperson to understand.
- This section should focus on the advantages of the invention and how it is different from the existing prior art.

It is also important to remember that the object of the invention should be consistent with the claims, and should not be worded in a way that limits the scope of the invention.

In summary, the object of the invention is an important section in a patent specification as it clearly communicates the solution sought by the invention and the specific technical problems it aims to solve. By emphasizing the main objective of the invention, discussing the advantages of the invention, and clearly stating the solution sought, this section can effectively convey the inventive nature of the invention to the patent office.

CHAPTER VIII

Summary of Invention

The summary of invention, also commonly referred to as the statement of invention, is a crucial section of a patent application. It puts forth the distinguishing novel features of an invention for which patent protection is desired. The goal of writing this section is to provide an accurate, readable, informative, understandable, and very concise description of the invention.

The Summary or the "Statement of invention" provides the essence of the entire inventive subject matter. It includes a description of the broadest possible protection that can be accorded to the invention. One possible method of writing the summary is to provide a readable non-legal form of the broadest independent claim.

This section should aim at stating the exact nature, operation and purpose of the invention. It should avoid labelling anything as "the invention", including the title of the section itself. For instance, it is preferable to use "Summary" rather than "Summary of the invention" as a title of this section. The section should not recite advantages and limiting objectives of the invention or any other matter that might limit the scope of the invention. It should not include any legal or claim language and should be broad enough such that alternative embodiments and implementations for the same or more elements are possible for the invention.

Best practices for writing the summary of invention include:

- Stating the exact nature, operation and purpose of the invention that would be of assistance in future patent searches.
- Avoiding the use of the term "the invention", including in the title of the section. For example, it is preferable to use "Summary" rather than "Summary of the invention" as the title.
- Avoiding the recitation of advantages and limiting objectives of the invention or any other matter that might limit the scope of the invention.
- Not including any legal or claim language.
- Keeping the statement broad enough such that alternative embodiments and implementations for the same or more elements are possible for the invention.

When writing the summary, it is also important to keep in mind the following guidelines:

- The summary should generally cover paraphrased independent claims.
- Dependent claims may also be included.
- The summary should start with a phrase like "In an aspect of this invention, a method and system for ....is provided".
- To add more points from other independent claims, use "in another aspect of this invention,".
- Avoid using "wherein", "said" in the summary.

An example of a summary of invention could be:

In an aspect of this invention, a method and system for a soil-based planting system is provided. The method includes the steps of preparing a soil mixture, planting seeds in the mixture, and providing the necessary water and nutrients for the growth of the plants. In another aspect of this invention, a new and improved gel-based planting system is provided. The gel-based system includes a gel matrix that holds the seeds and provides the necessary water and nutrients for the growth of the plants.

In conclusion, the summary of invention is a crucial section of a patent application that provides a concise and accurate description of the invention. It is important to follow best practices and guidelines when writing the summary to ensure that the invention is effectively communicated to the patent office and potential licensees or manufacturers.

It's important to remember that the summary should be consistent with the claims and should not be worded in a way that limits the scope of the invention. It should provide a broad and general overview of the invention, while still being

CHAPTER IX

Brief Description of Drawings

Brief Description of Drawings

Drawings are an important part of a patent specification as they can help to clearly and effectively illustrate the various embodiments and implementations of an invention. The drawings are usually accompanied by a brief description that provides a summary of what each drawing represents. The brief description should be clear, concise and easy to understand, and it should avoid using terms that may limit the scope of the invention. In this chapter, we will discuss the importance of drawings, best practices for creating drawings, and how to write a brief description of drawings.

Importance of Drawings

Drawings are considered to be part of a patent specification and the same may be supplied by the Applicant without being required by the Controller, and must be supplied if required by the Controller along with any specification, whether complete or provisional. Drawings are an essential element of the patent specification as they provide a visual representation of the invention. Drawings can help to illustrate the various features and aspects of an invention that would otherwise be difficult to describe in words. They can help to clearly and effectively communicate the invention to the patent office and to potential licensees or manufacturers.

Creating Drawings

When creating drawings, it is important to use standard A4 size sheets with a clear margin of at least 4 cm on the top and left hand and 3 cm at the bottom and right hand of every sheet. Drawings should be clear and easy to understand, and they should show the invention clearly without the need to mark dimensions on the drawings. Drawings or sketches that require a special illustration of the invention should be on separate sheet(s) and should not be self-explanatory. Sketches and rough drawings that were prepared as prerequisites to the patent preparation process can be used while making the drawings for the invention.

Whenever a patent application includes drawings, a brief description of each drawing needs to be enclosed in the respective specification. The patent office reviews the patent specification, including the brief description, to determine whether all the drawings that are described in the specification are present along with the application. The description should avoid using terms whose interpretation may limit the scope of invention, and no descriptive matter shall appear on the drawings except in the flow diagrams.

The brief description of each figure should be provided in a separate section, and it should be of 1-3 lines. The description should use bold font for the "FIG. X", and it should be followed by a semicolon (;) after the brief description of each figure, starting from the first. The last figure description should be followed by "semicolon + and". The brief description is generally the first line of each figure's detailed description.

Examples of Brief Description:

- FIG. 1 illustrates a conventional soil-based planting system, in accordance with an embodiment of the present disclosure;
- FIG. 2 illustrates a new and improved gel-based planting system, in accordance with an embodiment of the present disclosure;
- FIG. 3 illustrates a portable assembly for holding the gel-based planting system, in accordance with an embodiment of the present disclosure;
- FIG. 4 illustrates an isometric view of the portable assembly for holding the gel-based planting system, in accordance with an embodiment of the present disclosure; and
- FIG. 5A and FIG. 5B illustrate tables showing composition of soilless mixture, in accordance with various embodiments of the present disclosure.

In summary, the brief description of drawings is an important part of a patent specification, as it provides a summary of the visual representation of the invention. It is important to use standard A4 size sheets, clear and easy-to-understand drawings, and a clear and concise brief description to effectively communicate the invention to the patent office and to potential licensees or manufacturers. It is also important to follow the best practices and guidelines provided by the patent office when creating and describing the drawings. Properly created and described drawings can play a critical role in the success of a patent application. It is important to work closely with a patent attorney or agent to ensure that the drawings are in compliance with all the relevant regulations and guidelines. Overall, the brief description of drawings is an important aspect of patent drafting, and it should be given due consideration and attention to ensure that the patent application is complete and effective.

CHAPTER X

Detailed Description of Invention

The detailed description of invention, also known as the specification, is an essential part of a patent application. In complete specification detailed description of an invention contains enough detail in order to provide a complete picture of the invention. It ought to be composed in such a manner such that the individual who has ordinary aptitude in the art ought to have the capacity to do the creation without making extraordinary endeavors.

Irrespective of whether the Application is accompanied by either provisional or complete specification, description of invention must accompany. It should start on the different page. Provisional specification does not need to whereas complete specification needs to fully and particularly describe the invention and its operation or use and the method by which it is to be performed. Further, the detailed description part should disclose the best method of performing the invention which is known to the applicant and for which he is entitled to claim protection.

For explaining, best mode requirement for chemical reaction involving heating at specific temperature, it may not be required to disclose the exact degree of temperature, however a narrow range covering the exact temperature must be disclosed. The best mode requirement does not require applicants to disclose absolutely the best way of carrying out an invention but surely requires key aspects not to be kept secret.

A specification in respect of a divisional application must contain specific reference to the number of the original application from which the divisional application is made. A specification in respect of a patent of addition must contain a specific reference to the number of the main patent, or the application for the main patent, as the case may be, and a definite statement that the invention comprises an improvement in, or a modification of, the invention claimed in the specification of the main patent granted or applied for.

Description should not contain any Irrelevant or other matter not necessary for the elucidation of the Invention.

Additional requirement to be complied for invention mentioning biological materials: If an applicant mentions a biological material in a specification which may not be described in such a way as to fully and particularly describe the invention and its operation or use and the method by which it is to be performed and to disclose the best method of performing the invention which is known to the applicant for which he is entitled to claim protection and if such material is not available to the public, the application shall be completed by depositing the material to an international depository authority under the Budapest Treaty and by fulfilling the following conditions, namely:

(A) the deposit of the material shall be made not later than the date of filing the patent application in India and a reference thereof shall be made in the specification within three months from the date of filing of the application; The following two institutes have acquired the status of international depositary authority (IDA) under the Budapest Treaty in India:

1. International Depositary Authority, Microbial Culture Collection (MCC), National Centre for Cell Science (NCCS), University of Pune Campus, Ganesh Hind, Pune-411007, Maharashtra.
2. International Depositary Authority, Microbial Type Culture Collection and Gene Bank (MTCC), Institute of Microbial Technology (IMTECH), Council of Scientific and Industrial Research (CSIR), Sector 39-A, Chandigarh.

(B) all the available characteristics of the material required for it to be correctly identified or indicated are included in the specification including the name, address of the depository institution and the date and number of the deposit of the material at the institution; and

(C) Disclose the source and geographical origin of the biological material in the specification, when used in an invention.

Detailed description section follows the summary section of a patent specification and completely describes the invention under consideration. Description of the invention includes a written disclosure of the invention, drawings, and one or more claims that define the scope of protection for the invention. It is important to draft the specification in a clear and concise manner, with sufficient detail to enable a person having ordinary skill in the art to understand, make, and use the invention. The claims should be drafted as broadly as possible, while still being fully supported by the written description of the invention.

In summary, the detailed description of invention is an essential part of a patent application. It includes a written description of the invention and one or more claims that define the scope of protection for the invention. It is important to draft the specification in a clear and concise manner, with sufficient detail to enable a person having ordinary skill in the art to understand, make, and use the invention. The claims should be drafted as broadly as possible, while still being fully supported by the written description of the invention. Additionally, if the invention mentions biological materials, the applicant must comply with the additional requirements set forth by the Budapest Treaty, including depositing the material with an International Depository Authority and disclosing certain information in the specification.

Detailed description section follows the summary section of a patent specification and completely describes the invention under consideration. Description of the invention includes a written disclosure that explains, in clear and concise terms, how to make and practice the invention so as to support the working of the invention. The detailed description is written such that it is understood by anyone who possesses ordinary skill in the art and can use the invention. The detailed description should enable an ordinary person to develop the necessary technical know-how to make the invention work.

The section should disclose the details of the invention such that the best mode to practice the inventive concept is clearly laid out. The nature of improvements or modifications of the invention with respect to the prior art should be clearly and sufficiently described. The section should clearly highlight the preferred embodiment(s) of the invention. A preferred embodiment is a physical structure of the invention and refers to how various elements of the invention connect with each other to perform the desired job. In case the invention is a process, the method of conducting the invention should be described.

Each invention can have multiple embodiments that describe one or more structures possible for the invention. For instance, consider that an invention pertains to a compression algorithm to be used over a computer network. In one embodiment, the compressed data can be passed through a connection oriented protocol, such as TCP, and in another embodiment, the data can be passed through a connectionless protocol such as UDP.

As mentioned before, the detailed description should describe the best mode of practicing an invention. The best mode doesn't need to be literally the most efficient way of carrying out the invention, but should rather mention what the inventor believes to be the best method known at the time of filing the patent application. In case the inventor finds out a better way of carrying out the invention after the filing, it's generally not compulsory to add the new mode to the patent specification unless the examiner explicitly asks for it. Furthermore, in case a patent specification includes several modes of carrying out an invention, some of which are more preferred than others, the patent specification does not need to indicate which mode the inventor considers to be the best mode.

Each invention can have one or more implementations. An implementation depicts multiple features of an invention and how various elements of that feature combine together to show the desired effect. For instance, computer processors can have multiple implementations for the purpose of providing the desired performance and are available at different pricing options. A processor architecture that supports a particular instruction set may have a first-level cache in one implementation, and may have both first and second level cache in another implementation.

Therefore, in cases where an invention has multiple implementations of carrying out the single inventive concept, it's beneficial to incorporate and describe all possible implementations to broaden the scope of the invention. However, care should be taken to make sure that each implementation points out to the same inventive concept. Inclusion of an implementation that functions away from what the inventive subject matter teaches would get a rejection based on the unity of invention.

The detailed description should support every element and feature that needs to be protected in the patent application. The invention should also fulfil the criterion of enablement, wherein the invention is described to the extent necessary to be enabling and with sufficient detail as to satisfy the written description requirement. For meeting the enabling requirement, the inventor must describe the manner and the process of making and using the invention to enable a person with ordinary skill in the art to practice it. However, the detailed description should not contain unnecessary terms and language that may be interpreted to limit the scope of the invention. For instance, terms such as "best", "special", "suitable" should be avoided. Also, statements that describe the invention as a whole rather than one embodiment at a time are more likely to limit the scope of protection. Therefore, it is always preferable to describe every structural aspect of the invention as an embodiment.

The detailed description section gives a complete picture of the invention. The detailed description can start with an overview of the invention and can clarify improvements and modifications of the invention over the prior art. The detailed description section can then describe multiple embodiments and implementations of the invention with respect to various structural and functional aspects, respectively. The description should be such that it is sufficient for an average person skilled in the art to perform the invention by developing the necessary technical know-how by himself.

Some key practices to be kept in mind while drafting the section are:

a. Write the overview as a brief description of the main embodiment of the invention.
b. Completely explain one element before moving onto a new or any other element in the description section. This helps to maintain readability.
c. Write the detailed description section, as for other sections, in clear and plain English. No section other than claims should use any legal language and should be easy to interpret and understand.
d. Use short and simple sentences. Short and plain sentences are preferred over long run-on or compound sentences.
e. Avoid writing any statement that may later be interpreted to have a negative connotation.
f. Also terms such as "always", "simultaneously", "essentially" should be avoided.
g. Maintain correct numbering of paragraphs. The paragraphs should be short and logically sequenced.

Support each term and technical jargon by broad based definitions. Each term should clearly bring out the necessity of the terminology used and why it is needed while protecting the invention.

h. Use each term and technical jargon consistently throughout the specification.
a. Terminologies that are not well known in the art should, whenever being introduced, should be clearly defined.
b. Broadening language should be used consistently across the description. However, it needs to be understood that the usage of broadening language does not implicitly cover alternative embodiments.
c. Disclose the best mode of carrying out the invention in the description. The best mode is the most effective way, which the inventor knows at the time of filing the patent application, of practicing the invention.
d. Verify that the application contains adequate details for one with ordinary skill in the technology to make and use the invention through the disclosed mode. For chemical and pharmaceutical applications, this verification can focus on any novel constituents and synthetic processes.

Do's and don'ts for Detailed Description:

- Follow strict antecedent basis. For example: a system xyz for the first time, the system xyz for the further usage.
- Don't use "wherein", "comprises", "consists", "comprising", instead use "include".
- Give examples.
- Use consistent numbering. For example-System 100, 102, 104... or 100, 105, 110... or 100, 110, 120.. For fig. 1 explanation and system 200, 202, 204.. Or 200, 205, 210... or 200, 210, 220. For fig. 2 explanation and the like.
- Don't use passive voice.
- Don't use pronouns.
- Don't use long sentences, except for examples.
- Explain each and every detail of the invention in the Specifications.
- Strictly Implement claims.

CHAPTER XI

Claims of Invention

Claims are an essential component of a patent application and serve as the legal definition of the invention. They define the boundaries of the scope of protection provided by the patent and are of paramount importance in both patent prosecution and litigation. Careful drafting of claims is crucial to ensure that they accurately reflect the invention and provide adequate protection while also distinguishing the invention from the prior art.

Claims must define the technical aspects of the invention and not its commercial advantages. They should be written in a specific format, using clear and precise language that is supported by the specification. They should also be self-contained and define at least one embodiment of the invention. Ideally, claims should also protect the invention itself, so that no physical embodiments of the invention can be made, used, or sold without infringing the claims.

It is the responsibility of the patent agent to draft claims that are as broad as necessary while also ensuring that they are genuine in light of the subject matter. Claims must comply with section 10(5) of the patent law, which states that they must relate to a single invention or a group of inventions linked by a single inventive concept.

Broad claims have the advantage of providing greater protection, but they may also attract objections based on prior art. Narrower claims, on the other hand, may be easier to design around for competitors.

To infringe a patent, the infringing invention must have at least all the elements of the claim. However, having more elements does not negate infringement, but having fewer elements does. Therefore, it is important to draft claims with a minimum number of elements to allow for the broadest possible protection.

It is important to understand the distinction between an invention, an embodiment, and claims.

Invention: An invention refers to the mental construct inside the mind of the inventor, which is intangible and has no physical form. It is a novel idea or solution to a known problem.

Embodiment: An embodiment, on the other hand, is the physical form of the invention that showcases its functionality to the world.

Claims: Claims, meanwhile, set the boundaries of the scope of protection for the invention as seen by the inventor and filed in the patent application. Upon grant of the patent, these claims provide protection to the inventor by excluding others from making, using, selling, or importing the invention.

It is crucial to remember that claims must meet the requirement of the patent office, i.e. they must "define the matter for which protection is sought; be clear and concise; and be supported by the description." Additionally, claims must also be drafted in such a way that they are not easily circumvented by potential infringers. This can be achieved by including all the essential elements of the invention and by avoiding the inclusion of unnecessary elements.

In conclusion, claims are a vital component of a patent application. They define the scope of protection provided by the patent and are crucial in both patent prosecution and litigation. Careful drafting of claims is essential to ensure that they accurately reflect the invention and provide adequate protection while also distinguishing the invention from the prior art.

Claims in a granted patent serve as the defining characteristic of the invention, outlining the scope of protection the inventor holds as their exclusive property. It is the duty of the patent agent to draft these claims as broadly as necessary, while still accurately and clearly describing the invention. The claims should be clear and concise and must be supported by the description provided in the specification. The scope of the patent monopoly is solely determined by the wording of the claims.

Well-drafted patents typically have a small number of short claims, as they provide the broadest coverage for the invention while using the minimum number of elements. The use of broad and inclusive language, such as the term "plurality" rather than a specific number, can aid in this endeavor. Additionally, reciting elements as "means plus a specific function" can broaden the scope of the claims and increase the chances of infringement.

It is important to note that the claims must recite the novelty aspect of the invention in a clear and fully supported manner, and should lead to a significant and unobvious result. The wording of the claims should also be clear and unambiguous to avoid potential misinterpretations during the patent examination process.

The sentence of the claim has generally three parts:

1. The Preamble
2. The Elements (claim body); and
3. The Interconnections (transition terms)

Structure of Claims

1. Each claim is to be in form of a single sentence.
2. The claim should begin with "I claim" or "The Invention claimed is" or something similar.
3. A claim should be begin with a capital letter and end with a period (full stop, inverted coma etc.)
4. Verb forms should be matching throughout the claims.

E.g.: Correct: A pencil having a fastener at one end

Incorrect: A pencil will have a fastener at one end or A pencil will have has a fastener at one end

Numbering

1. The broadest claim should be ordered first
2. Patent with one claim should not include numbers but multiple claims should be numbers consecutively.
3. Similar claims should be grouped together. If both product and processes are being claimed together, then the claim of each concept should be grouped together, i.e. all product claims be put together and all process claims be put together separately. The numbering of each concept be done consecutively.

Eg: Product Claim group 2,3,4,5; Process Claim group: 6,7,8,9

Preamble

a. Every claim starts with an introductory section called a "Preamble" indicating the statutory classes of the invention and describing it as a whole.
b. Short preamble is preferred.
c. The title of the invention introduces the invention.

Though it is preferred that it is chosen to be similar to the preambles of the claims, but can vary as needed, since the title is not read as claims limitation.

d. The preamble should be consistent with the scope of the actual claims, and should be revised if the scope of the claim is modified.
e. The preamble must match the invention described in the specification: if the specification calls for a pencil, the claims should not specify writing instrument; similarly, if the invention is useful on pencil or pen, the claim should not specify pencil.
f. The preamble should not include unnecessary limitation. The preamble being the introductory section of the claims, does not become a limitation, if it simply states the intended use or purpose of the invention. If the claim body recites a structurally complete invention that does not need the preamble language for support, the preamble is not limiting. The determination of whether a preamble limits a claim is made on a case-by-case basis in light of the facts of each case. The claim preamble must be read in the context of the entire claim. Any terminology in the preamble that limits the structure of the claim of the invention. The determination of whether preamble

recitations are structural limitations can be resolved only on review of the entirely of the application to gain an understanding of what the inventors actually invented and intended to be encompassed by the claim.

g. Hence, if a limitation is necessary for the claims to be patentable, it should be included in the body of the claims, perhaps in a "whereby" clause.

Only, the invention where limitation is needed to put the rest of the claims in proper and understandable context, it can be featured in the preamble e.g. In composition of matter claims that describe a new and unnamed material, the preamble could be "a composition comprising materials Y and Z whereby the composition has density W and color X".

h. Since, dependent claims implicitly includes the text of the parent claims, the limitation of the preamble of the parent claim also becomes the limitation of the dependent claim. It is incorrect to specify an invention in a dependent claim that is broader in any aspect than its parent claims.
i. The Patent office relies on the preamble to the application for making to an appropriate examining group, so changing the claims with this goal in the mind is helpful. E.g. in one instance, the application load on microprocessor group was less than the software group, the preamble was changed from software to microprocessor to get the application marked to the microprocessor group.

Transition Term:

a. are the words between the preamble and claim body. The two most common transition terms: "comprising and consisting of" are used to describe sub- elements in a claim and are similarly interpreted in that context.
b. Transition Term "comprising" mean "including the following elements but not excluding others". The synonymous words such as "including", having "containing", "wherein" etc. can also be used but these terms may be construed as less open than "comprising", "wherein" etc. can also be used but these terms may be construed as less open than "comprising"

e.g.: An apparatus, comprising: a pencil; an eraser attached to one end of the pencil; and a grip attached to the center of the pencil.

c. Transmission terms "consisting of" means "including the following elements, no more and no less". term The are synonymous composed of "constituting" and "being". A claim "consisting of certain elements may contain trace amounts of other non - functional elements, but no more than that.

e.g. An apparatus, consisting of: a pencil; an eraser attached to the pencil; and a grip attached to the pencil.

Though there is no difference in dictionary meaning of these two words "Comprises " and "Consisting", but in patent practice these words have different interpretations. 'Comprising' denotes a very broad and open claim which can be interpreted to include unspecified ingredients, even in major amounts.

'Consisting' of would generally imply a narrow claim not allowing inclusion of materials other than those already stated in the claims. "Comprising" or "Comprises" is the most preferred transitional word for most situations. The use of word imply that the considered device has at least the list of things which follow "comprising" but might have other things also.

Let us take examples. Two claims are stated in the following. manner;

Claim 1 A writing instrument, which comprises a pencil and clip for holding the apparatus in a product, said clip being attached to said pencil.

This claim covers all writing instruments which have at least a pencil and a clip. A writing instrument containing other elements, such as an eraser attached to the pencil will be covered under this claim. The claim has become very broad by the use of the word 'comprises'.

Claim 2 A pharmaceutical composition which consists of the anti-malarial agent Y and a pharmaceutically acceptable carrier.

In this case, the claim covers compositions which contain only anti-malarial agent Y and the carrier and nothing else. A composition which contains any additional ingredients does not infringe the claim.

Example: A chair comprising of a seat, a back and four legs.

"Consisting of" The device would have the following list of elements and nothing else. A device. which has components infringe. additional will not.

Example: A chair consisting of a seat, a back and four legs.

A claim will cover only these elements. Adding anything such as leg stand will not infringe the chair covered by the claim.

"Consisting essentially of" - The device has the following list, and possibly some unimportant other things which do not materially affect the basis and novel.

Example: A chair consisting essentially of a seat, a back and four legs.

The scope of this claim is not really clear. The device could cover unimportant additives such as paint or polish. Adding adjustable back change mechanism, the will basic characteristics of the chair. Do not use this transition word if it is avoidable.

The transition term " consisting essentially of" is a slightly broader version of "consisting of" which allows the addition of elements that do not affect the basic and novel characteristics of the invention.

It is typically used for composition of matter, but may also be used in methods. Synonymous word:

"composed of", "consisting prevailingly but not essentially of".

"Having", "Composed of" It is best not to use these transitional words as their scope of meaning is open to interpretation by the Examiner as well as courts. And their interpretation will necessarily have to be done after considering the specifications to determine whether other elements are included or not. And their conclusion may be at variance from the meaning the inventor intended leading to an inimical effect on the claims.

"Including", "containing" or "Characterized by" are equivalent to "comprising" but are not preferred.

Claim Body

1. The body of a claim recites the element of the claim and describes how they cooperate structurally, physically, or functionally to form an operative invention.
2. Elements that do not cooperate in same fashion are at best an 'aggregate' and usually are not accepted
3. The claim language should be technical but not laudatory or surplus

e.g. " a hand held writing instrument comprising writing an element, thus to write darker than before". (the later clause should be deleted)

d. Where the invention is a single element e.g. a pure composition, it is simply described.
e. Claim elements are usually respected as a list. The element can be separated by commas or semicolons or feature an outline style, prefacing each claims element with (a), (b), (c) etc. The later forum is helpful for claims that refer back to previous elements ("after step (c)").

Types of claims based on the type of invention:

1. **Apparatus or device claims:** An apparatus or device claim protects embodiments of an invention in the form of a physical apparatus, system, or device.
2. **Method claims or process claims:** Method claims are claims that recite a sequence of steps that together complete a task such as making an article of some sort.
3. **Composition claims:** Claims related to compositions are used where the invention to be claimed has to do with the chemical nature of the materials or components used.

Unity of Invention and Clarity of Claims:

Claim(s) of a complete specification shall relate to a single invention, or to a group of inventions linked so as to form a single inventive concept. Claims shall be clear and succinct and fairly based on the matter disclosed in the specification.

Claims Sets:

Claims can be both independent and dependent. An independent claim is the broadest claim. Each dependent claim is the broadest claim. Each dependent claim refers to an independent claim and includes all of its features, and then adds further details to the independent claim.

The claims of the patent must have at least one independent claim.

1. Independent Claims

Independent claim defines the invention in the broadest/widest scope possible. As the name implies, independent claims stand alone and do not need to be read with other claims in order to interpret them.

Each claim set always begins with an independent claim. However, a patent may have more than one independent claim provided the unity of invention aspect is taken care of. For example, if the invention contains various embodiments and such embodiments cannot be covered by one broad independent claim, then the patent specification may contain more than one independent claim.

The broadest independent claim which is usually the first claim should not be too long. Because writing a long claim will necessarily have lots of limitations which could create opportunities for infringement. The infringer can usually change his product in some minor way to avoid the inherent limitations to avoid infringement.

2. Dependent Claims

Dependent claims are the claims that depend upon a preceding claims; the preceding claim may be an independent claim or a dependent claim. These claims are used to add further limitations to the preceding claim. Dependent claims generally claim additional features of the independent claim or further define a feature of the independent claim. A dependent claim has to the read in conjunction with the claim on which it depends. Hence, if you see a patent claim states

"The machine of Claim1," the claim is a dependent claim that includes all of the limitations of the claim or claims upon which it depends. In other words, the independent claim is abroad claim, while the dependent claim narrows the independent claim.

a. A dependent claim cannot be infringed without the parent claims being infringed or putting in another way the independent claim must be infringed if its dependent claim is infringed.
b. Each dependent claim should begin by referring to the basic claim or a previous dependent claim. If the dependent claim recites one or more elements of the independent claim more narrowly, it should use the word wherein, if the dependent claim recites additional elements, it should use the words "further comprising", and then continue by reciting the additional features of the invention. The additional features can be those which were eliminated in broadening the basic claims and all other subsidiary features, including all combinations and permutations of features of the invention. A dependent claim must recite the elements of its parent claim more specifically, or recite additional elements. It may not change any element to a different type or kind.
c. The preamble of a dependent claim should clarify the dependency.

("the apparatus of claim, wherein..........")

But the dependency may also be specified elsewhere in the dependent claim.

("a combination comprising(x), and the apparatus of claim1, connected to (x)")

d. A dependent claim is construed as if it incorporated all the limitations of the claim to which it refers. For example, if the independent claim recites a chair

with an adjustable back and the dependent claims reads "the chair of claim 1 with adjustable back connected by a 5m connected rod", the dependent claim doesn't claim the chair with adjustable back per se, but rather the 5m connecting rod in combination with chair with an adjustable back. Thus if the independent claim recites a table having a top and the dependent claim reads "the table of claim 1, wherein said top has multiple channels", the dependent claim doesn't claim the top with channels per se, but rather the top with channels in combination with table.

e. It is preferable to place all claim dependent on an independent claim before the next independent claim.
f. Dependent claims are useful to explain and differentiate (broaden) abstract terms of the independent claims. They are useful to provide a specific descriptive recitation. For example, acidic means in parent claim can be qualified to mean acid or solutions of specific pH values recited through the dependent claims.

1. **Multiple dependent claims:**

This is another form of the dependent claim. A "multiple dependent claims" refers to two or more previous claims in the alternative.

e.g. ("the apparatus of claim 1 or 2 further comprising..........")

If the alternative is not mentioned, then it is not allowed.

e.g. ("an apparatus according to claims 1-3......")

A multiple dependent claim cannot refer to any other multiple dependent claim.

Construction of Claims:

Claims are written as a single sentence in a precise language. There are many facts features that need to be considered while writing claim. Some of the facts are described below:

Parts of the Claim

A patent claim constitutes three parts

1. **The preamble:** It is an introductory and expressionary statement that sets the limits of the invention in a broad manner. It identifies the category and purpose of the invention, like whether the invention is related to an article, a device, an apparatus, a composition/formulation, a method or a process. The preamble can be considered as simple definition of the invention to be claimed. It is usually not considered to be a legally limiting constraint on the invention.
2. **The transitional phrase:** It is used to link the preamble to the patent claim of the specific elements. The transitional phrase is of two types:

- **Open-ended transitional phrase:** It gives the claim an interpretation of including the stated elements of the invention but not excluding the other additional elements. Examples of open-ended transitional phrases are "comprising", "including", "containing", etc.
- **Close-ended transitional phrase:** It gives an interpretation of "being limited to nothing more than one specifically-recited elements in the claims. Examples of close-ended transitional phrases are "consisting of" "consisting essentially of".

3. **The body of the claim**: It explains the invention's elements and their relationship with each other. It has various elements of the invention that depends on the kind of invention. If the invention is related to a device, then the body would define the various parts, their functions in some sort of logical order and how they are connected to each other. Finally, the claims to a method invention will list the procedure generally in order in which they are

to be carried out.

Claim Punctuation:

Every patent office has strict requirements of how a claim should be punctuated in order to avoid incorrect interpretation of the claim. It is important that the instructions of the patent office are strictly adhered to:

- A coma is used to separate the preamble from the transitional phrase and a colon separated the transitional phrase from the body.
- The body may be divided into various sub-paragraphs that define the elements of the claim and the penultimate element of a claim ends with "and".
- Other punctuations such as parentheses, dashes, quotation marks etc. are not generally used in writing the claim.

Antecedent Basis

The first time an element or part is mentioned to in a claim set, the indefinitely article 'a' or 'an' is to be used and when the element is mentioned again in the claims, the definite article 'the' or 'said' should be used. In each claim set the antecedent basis needs to be re-established. Lack of antecedent basis can lead to claim scope being indefinite.

Below are given some examples of claims to make the claim construction and kinds of claims clearer.

Independent Claim

1. A motor vehicle for transporting people and objects, having a chassis and a body mounted on the chassis, the motor vehicle comprising:

a. a plurality of wheels under the body; supporting the chassis;
b. a transmission mounted on the chassis and coupled to at least one of the plurality of wheels;
c. a motor mounted on the chassis, having a fluid input and an output coupled to the transmission; and
d. a fluid supply mounted within the body, coupled to the fluid input of the motor by a portoflan armature coupled to the fluid supply, a gronk tube coupled to the fluid input of the motor; and a variable orifice between the portoflan armature and the gronk tube.

The preamble, in this case, is: "A motor vehicle...."

The connecting word or the "transitional phrase" is: "comprising", and

The body of claim lists the four elements and their inter-relationship so as to make the motor vehicle functional namely – wheels, a transmission, a motor and a fluid supply.

Please note that the proper antecedent basis has been taken care of in this claim. For example, a plurality of wheels when they are referred to again in part (b), the definite article 'the' has been used.

Dependent Claim:

2. The motor vehicle of claim 1, in which the fluid supply is a tank of compressed gas, and the motor is a variable-displacement fluid motor.

The preamble, in this case, is: "The motor vehicle of claim 1" Please note that in the dependent claim of this claim set, the proper antecedent basis has been taken care of. For example, when 'motor vehicle' and 'fluid supply tank' have been referred to here, the definite article 'the' has been used.

Specific type of claims:

1. **Invention based patent claims**

Patent claims can be classified on the basis of invention as : Product Claim, Process or method claim, Apparatus or Device Claim

Product Claim: The claim which claims the actual product of the invention is called Product Claim. For example: a chemical compound, compound used as pharmaceuticals, composition mixtures such as alloy, food, drink etc.

A pharmaceutical composition comprising:

An amido-amine polymer comprising an amido-amine dendrimer derived from:

i. A multi-amine; and
ii. A multifunctional compound comprising two or more amine-reactive groups; and
iii. A pharmaceutically acceptable excipient.

The product claim includes a substance or compositions (e.g. a chemical compound) as well as any physical entity (e.g., object, article, apparatus, machine or system of co-operating apparatus) which is produced by a person's technical skill. Examples are:

i. a steering mechanism incorporating an automatic feed-back circuit...
ii. a woven garment comprising.....
iii. a communication system comprising a plurality of transmitting and receiving stations; and
iv. an insecticides consisting of X, Y, Z.

Process Claim: The claim which claims a new process or method to achieve the desired result is called Process Claim. For example: methods of preparation, methods of analysis, method of treatment etc.

The process or method claim is applicable to all kinds of activities in which the use of some material product for effecting the process is implied; the activity may be exercised upon material products, upon energy, upon other processes (as in control process) or upon living things.

Method claims are claims that recites a sequence of steps which together complete a task such as making an article of some sort. An example of a method claim is as follows:

A method for making tea, the method comprising:

a. boiling water:
b. adding sugar to the boiled water;
c. adding tea leaves to the boiling water to form a mixture;
d. adding milk to mixture; and
e. filtering mixture.

A bio-assisted method for treatment of hydrocarbon-contaminated soil employing a blend of selective microbes, the method comprising; isolating the microbes, which are capable of releasing oil from contaminated soil/gravel particles, adding the isolated microbes into said soil to release the oils, adding separately isolated microbes, which are capable of degrading the released oils, providing optimized nutrient for the microorganisms, and the aerating the same by periodic mixing of the oil contaminated soil-water slurry or by air sparging to treat the contaminated soil.

Method or process claims will include active steps to achieve a certain result. In method claims the transition is typically either "comprising" or "comprising the steps of". While legally there may be some distinction between these two different transitions, both are acceptable.

Apparatus Claim:

The product claim claimed for a device or a system or an article is called 'Apparatus Claim'. An apparatus or device claim protects embodiments of an invention in the form of a physical apparatus, system or a device. For instance, a claim that covers a tripod for a camera or a window crank is an apparatus claim. When drafting an apparatus claim, we can begin by reciting in a preamble what that apparatus is and what it does next. We can list the essential items of an invention. Essential elements are ones required for the functioning of the inventive device in its most basic form. E.g. the essence of the invention. The novelty of the invention lies in the essential components.

Examples for apparatus claim are:

An apparatus for supporting a camera, comprising a pivotal mounting configured to hold the camera; and a plurality of legs arranged to support the pivotal mounting.

In the example, the preamble recites that it is an apparatus for supporting a camera. The body of the claim recites that the essential elements of this apparatus are a pivotal mounting for the camera and legs arranges to support the pivotal mounting.

Field Based Patent Claims

Jepson Claim

Jepson claim style is used in the process or product claim where the invention is a modification or the improvement of the existing technology. The word "wherein"... often used to structure the Jepson Claim.

An assembly of blanks for a smoking article package comprising: an outer shell black comprising two major panels and two minor panels: and at least one inner compartment blank comprising two major panels and two minor panels; wherein a plurality of inner shells are formable from the at least one inner compartment blank.

Markush Claim

Markush Claim is generally used to structure the chemical invention where the composition of the invention has to be described in a structural diagram or formula based.

A compound having the formula: R-CH=N-S-X, where: R is an alkyl group selected from the group consisting of methyl, ethyl and isopropyl; and X is a halogen selected from the group consisting of chlorine and bromine.

Swiss Claim

The structure of claim used to claim the second or new medicinal use of the known substances or compositions is known as Swiss type Claim. India does not allow this type of claim under the provision of section 3 (d) of the Patent Act, 1970.

"Use of taxol and sufficient medications to prevent severe anaphylactic reactions, for manufacturing a medicamentation for simultaneous , separate, or sequential application of from 135mg/m2 up to 175mg/m2 taxol over a period of about 3 hours or less as a means for treating cancer and simultaneously reducing neutropenia.

Composition Claims

In this type of claim, components/ingredients used in the process are explained in the details which include their chemical nature, quantity used in the, manufacturing.

For example: A probiotic drink composition comprising of live bacteria (Lactobacillus casei Shirota), skimmed milk powder, sugar, glucose, water and more than 6.5 billion of live bacteria. Energy, Proteins, Carbohydrates, fat. The outcomes of claims majorly depends upon the information available in the prior art documents, scope of invention and other relevant factors.

Structure based Patent Claim

Pure Structure

A method of structuring claim where the part of an invention 'A' is structurally linked to the part 'B'. Example: A switch connected to a lamp

Means plus function

A method of structuring claim where the part of an invention 'A' is an element for achieving the part 'B'. Example: Means for signaling with a lamp

Structure is function

A method of structuring claim where invention defines structure and/or function.

Example: Signal Lamp

Pure Function

A method of structuring claim where the part of an invention 'A' is functioning with the part 'B'.

Example: Signaling lamp with the switch

Step plus function

A method of structuring claim where the part of an invention 'A' is a step for the function of part 'B'. Example: Step for signaling the lamp with the switch

Significance of Claims

a. A claim is a statement of technical facts expressed in legal terms defining the scope of the invention sought to be protected. No exclusivity is obtained for any matter described in the Complete Specification unless it is claimed in the claims.
b. What is not claimed in the 'claims' stand disclaimed, and is open to public use, even if the matter is disclosed in the description.
c. Claims define the boundaries of legal protection sought by the patentee and form a protective fence around the invention which is defined by the words and phrases in the claims.
d. The claims shall clearly define the scope of the invention with conciseness, precision and accuracy, so that others may know the exact boundary into which they should not trespass.
e. Each claim is evaluated on its own merit and, therefore, if one of the claims is objected, it does not mean.

Scope of Claims

a. Claims must not be too broad to embrace more than what the applicant has in fact invented. A Claim which is too broad may encroach upon the subject matter which is in public domain or belongs to others.
b. However, a claim may not be too narrow also because such a claim would not be sufficiently effective against potential infringement. An infringer would go scot-free, if the claims were too narrow and hence, the full benefit of the invention may not accrue to the inventor.
c. Having many claims, where each claim has a different scope, allows the applicant to have a legal title to different aspects of the invention. A good drafting may begin with broad claims and develops towards claims that are narrower in scope.
d. Terms of the claims which confuse the scope of the invention, or claims that are not specific (e.g. any novel matter) should be avoided.
e. A claim shall be for the protection of either a product or process, as the case may be, and shall be in one sentence according to the standard practice.

Following points should be considered while drafting patent claims

1. Each claim should be a single sentence and should be clearly worded.
2. Each claim should be precise and without unnecessary repetition.
3. Rights are given to claims only, not for any matter described in the complete specification.
4. Claims define the boundaries of legal protection and form a protective fence around the invention.
5. Each claim is evaluated on its own merit and, therefore, if one of the claims is objected, it does not mean that the rest of the claims are invalid.

Tips on Drafting Claims

1. Figure out all essential features or elements of your invention that you want to claims right to.
2. Start with broadest claims of your invention and then progress to narrower claims.
3. Start claims on a new page and number each claim using Arabic numbers starting with 1.
4. Precede your claims with a short statement such as "I/We claims:"
5. Be precise – the suggested way is

g. The first time any element is mentioned, the article "a" is used

h. When the element is referred to again by its original designation, "said" is used.
a. When another aspect of the element is referred – "the" is used.

6. It is important to ensure that any term being used in the claims has been clearly and purposefully described previously in the specification. This will avoid the possibility of any ambiguity in the interpretation of the term used. No abbreviation such as IP (Use "internet protocol") or relative terms such as greater (Use "greater than") be used.
7. Each claim should consist of an introduction, linking word, and body.
8. The first claim would be the independent claim and subsequent claim would be dependent claims and, these claims should be linked so as to form a single inventive concept.
9. There is no restriction to the number of claims to be incorporated in the specification. But, the applicant has to pay additional fee, if there are more than ten claims.
10. Claims must be supported by the description and if required may be presented through the drawings. This means that all the characteristics of the invention that form the part of the claims must be fully explained in the description.

Example: Claim for a Pencil(www.fishiplaw.com)

1. The invention claims a hand held writing instrument comprising a core element and a holder encapsulating the core element.

2. The invention of claim 1, wherein the core element is an element which leaves a mark when moved across on any paper or surface

3. The invention of claim 1, wherein the holder is made of material which prevents breakage and allows the means to hold conveniently.

4. The invention of claim 1 wherein an end of the holder can be removed to expose an end of said core element for writing.

Let us analyze the drafting of the above claim.

At the start we try to figure out what the invention does and what the invention really constitutes.

Claim 1: Independent claim. The interlinking word is "comprising" to give the impression that the invention has the mentioned essential elements but can have others also. Specifies the essentials. - core element and holder encapsulating the core element. The word core element is generalist to broaden the scope of claim. Core element could include writing elements such as lead, crayons, color or any other which leaves an impression when used. Similarly, holder could include wood, metal, plastic or anything rigid which can encapsulate the softer writing element.

(a) elongated core-element means that will leave a marking line if moved across paper or other similar surface, and

(b) an elongated holder surrounding and encasing said elongated core element one portion of said holder being removable from an end thereof to expose an end of said core element means so as to enable said core-element means to be exposed for writing,

whereby said holder protects said core element means from breakage and provides an enlarged means for holding said core element means conveniently.

Now that the basic theoretical aspects of the patent drafting has been covered, we can move on to actual drafting. For this, as a practical tool, a few questions are suggested which can be very useful especially to the beginners. The genesis of the suggested questions lies in various sub heads of the specification. The answers to these questions will help to understand the invention clearly in context of building up of specifications.

The Question Box

"The following questions are designed to help understand the invention and its potential for patent protection.

Invention-Focussed:

1. What is the invention about?

2. What problem does it claim to solve?
3. What solution does the invention provide?
4. What is the prior art related to the invention?
5. How is the invention better than the prior art?
6. What is the "novelty factor" or core concepts of the invention?
7. What is the suggested embodiment of the invention?

Inventor-Focused:

8. Does the inventor understand what he wants to protect?
9. What does the inventor believe to be the invention?

Competition-Focussed:

10. What is the competition or alternatives?
11. What are the ways the invention can be infringed?
12. How can the invention be achieved without infringing on existing patents?
13. Is it possible to reverse-engineer the invention? If so, what level of difficulty, cost, or hindrances are anticipated?

Drafting-Focussed:

14. How should the invention be claimed?"

CHAPTER XII

Abstract of Invention

The abstract of invention is a brief summary of the invention, which is included in a patent application as part of the specification. The abstract is intended to provide a quick and easy-to-read summary of the invention, allowing a patent examiner or other interested party to quickly understand the nature and scope of the invention.

The abstract is typically no more than 150 words in length and should be written in clear and concise language. It should provide a general overview of the invention, including its purpose and operation, and should not include any technical or legal jargon.

The abstract should begin by stating the technical field of the invention, followed by a brief statement of the problem or need that the invention addresses. Next, it should provide a summary of the invention's features and how they solve the problem or meet the need. Finally, it should provide a summary of the invention's advantages over the prior art.

It is important to note that the abstract is not a separate claim, it is only a summary of the invention and should not be used to define the scope of the claims. It should be written in a way that provides a general overview of the invention and not in a way that limits the scope of the invention.

In addition, when drafting the abstract, care should be taken to avoid including any information that is not covered in the specification or that is not supported by the claims. The abstract should be a true reflection of the invention as disclosed in the specification and should not include any new or additional information.

In conclusion, the abstract of invention is a brief summary of the invention that is included in a patent application as part of the specification. It should be written in clear and concise language, provide a general overview of the invention and should not include any technical or legal jargon. The abstract should not be used to define the scope of the claims and should be a true reflection of the invention as disclosed in the specification.

How to write Abstract?

- Abstract should not be more than 150 words.
- Abstract is written by paraphrasing independent claims only.
- In case of various independent claims, paraphrase only first and foremost important claim in abstract.
- Start the abstract with a phrase "The present invention provides a method and a system for".

Achieving Success On The Patent Agent Examination 2023

Congratulations on reaching the end of this book! We hope that you have found it to be a valuable resource in your preparation for the Patent Agent Examination 2023. By providing a comprehensive overview of the legal principles and practices related to patent drafting, along with practical tips and strategies for effectively navigating the exam, we have aimed to make this book an ideal study resource for busy professionals or anyone looking for a quick and efficient way to review the material.

As you prepare for the examination, remember to draw upon the knowledge and skills that you have gained from this book, as well as from your other studies and experiences. Trust in your own abilities and don't be afraid to ask for help if you need it. With hard work and determination, you can succeed on the Patent Agent Examination and embark on a rewarding and fulfilling career in intellectual property law.

We would like to thank you for choosing this book as your guide on this journey. We wish you the best of luck on the Patent Agent Examination and in all of your future endeavors.

We also recommend you to practice drafting and review as many patent applications as possible, this will help you to understand the nuances of patent drafting and will also help you to develop your own drafting skills.

In addition, we recommend that you seek out additional resources, such as workshops, webinars, and study groups, to supplement your studies and gain a more comprehensive understanding of the legal principles and practices related to patent drafting.

We hope that this book has been a valuable resource for your studies and has helped you develop a deeper understanding of the legal principles and practices governing the protection and enforcement of patents. We wish you all the best in your future endeavors as a patent agent.

9 798889 516927

Printed by Libri Plureos GmbH in Hamburg,
Germany